WISDOM

WISDOM

Warren W. Wiersbe

VICTOR BOOKS

A DIVISION OF SCRIPTURE PRESS PUBLICATIONS INC.
USA CANADA ENGLAND

Unless otherwise noted, Scripture quotations are from the *Holy Bible: New International Version®*. Copyright © 1973, 1978, 1984 by International Bible Society. Used by permission of Zondervan Publishing House. All rights reserved. Quotations marked KJV are from the *Authorized (King James) Version*.

Editor: Afton Rorvik
Designer: Grace K. Chan Mallette

Library of Congress Cataloging-in-Publication Data

Wiersbe, Warren W.
   Wisdom: a 30-day devotional / by Warren W. Wiersbe.
     p.   cm.
   Each devotional is adapted from a chapter in Be wise.
   ISBN 1-56476-404-4 (pbk.)
   1. Bible. N.T. Corinthians, 1st—Devotional literature.
2. Devotional calendars. I. Wiersbe, Warren W. Be wise. II. Title.
BS2675.4.W56 1995
227'.207—dc20   95-6247
                                                                                                                CIP

© 1995 by Victor Books/SP Publications, Inc. All rights reserved. Printed in the United States of America.

1 2 3 4 5 6 7 8 9 10 Printing/Year 99 98 97 96 95

No part of this book may be reproduced without written permission, except for brief quotations in books and critical reviews. For information write Victor Books, 1825 College Avenue, Wheaton, Illinois 60187.

If you are studying *Be Wise* in a Sunday School class or small group, this 30-Day Devotional will complement your study. Each devotional is adapted from a chapter in *Be Wise*. The following chart indicates the correlation. You may, of course, use this book without reference to *Be Wise*.

Be Wise **Wisdom**

Book Chapter	30-Day Devotional
1	Days 1, 2, and 3
2	Days 4, 5, and 6
3	Days 7 and 8
4	Days 9 and 10
5	Days 11, 12, and 13
6	Days 14 and 15
7	Days 16 and 19
8	Days 17 and 18
9	Days 20 and 21
10	Days 22 and 23
11	Days 24, 25, and 26
12	Days 27 and 28
13	Days 29 and 30

INTRODUCTION

We live in the midst of a "knowledge explosion" so incredible that even the experts can't keep up with all the developments in their fields. More and more, people are having to specialize, and the specialists have to depend on each other.

Knowledge abounds, but wisdom languishes. Wisdom is the right use of knowledge. Knowledge has to do with *facts*, but wisdom thrives on *truths.* Knowledge has to do with *facts*, but wisdom thrives on *truths.* Knowledge prepares you to make a living, but wisdom enables you to make a life. Our world is rich in knowledge and poor in wisdom; and, tragically enough, the world doesn't know where wisdom is found.

According to the Apostle Paul, true wisdom is found in Jesus Christ. When Paul wrote the letter we call First Corinthians, he wrote it for a group of Christians who were trying to mix Christian wisdom and pagan philosophy, the "wisdom of God" and the "wisdom of this world." Paul showed them how foolish they were in this attempt.

Paul explains in this letter what true wisdom is, how to get it, and how to use it to the glory of God and the building up of His church. If you want to "be wise," there's a price to pay; *but the price to pay for being foolish is even greater!*

First Corinthians is a letter about real people with real problems, a letter that magnifies Jesus Christ, the Cross, and the wisdom of God in Christ. It's a letter we all need to study today.

So, don't just get smart. Be wise.

—Warren W. Wiersbe

*My thanks to Stan Campbell,
who compiled the contents of this book
and added thought-provoking questions
to enrich your personal growth.*

DAY 1

Read *1 Corinthians 1:1-3*

Problems in the Church

"Jesus, yes! The church, no!"

Remember when that slogan was popular among young people in the 60s? They certainly could have used it with sincerity in Corinth back in A.D. 56, because the local church there was in serious trouble. Sad to say, the problems did not stay within the church family; they were known by the unbelievers outside the church.

To begin with, the church at Corinth was a *defiled* church. Some of its members were guilty of sexual immorality; others got drunk; still others were using the grace of God to excuse worldly living. It was also a *divided* church, with at least four different groups competing for leadership (1:12). This meant it was a *disgraced* church. Instead of glorifying God, it was hindering the progress of the Gospel.

How did this happen? The members of the church permitted the sins of the city to get into the local assembly. Corinth was a polluted city, filled with every kind of vice and worldly pleasure. It was also a proud, philosophical city, with many itinerant teachers promoting their speculations.

> *"To the church of God in Corinth, to those sanctified in Christ Jesus and called to be holy, together with all those everywhere who call on the name of our Lord Jesus Christ"*
>
> *(1 Corinthians 1:2).*

Any time you have proud people, depending on human wisdom, adopting the lifestyle of the world, you are going to have problems.

Applying God's Truth:

1. In what ways is your church like the church at Corinth? How is it different?

2. How is your church influenced by the problems of the city where it is located?

3. What, personally, do you hope to accomplish by reading through the Book of 1 Corinthians?

DAY 2

Read 1 Corinthians 1:4-17

Divided Loyalties

A Christian photographer friend told me about a lovely wedding that he "covered." The bride and groom came out of the church, heading for the limousine, when the bride suddenly left her husband and ran to a car parked across the street! The motor was running and a man was at the wheel, and off they drove, leaving the bridegroom speechless. The driver of the "get-away car" turned out to be an old boyfriend of the bride, a man who had boasted that "he could get her any time he wanted her." Needless to say, the husband had the marriage annulled.

When a man and woman pledge their love to each other, they are set apart for each other, and any other relationship outside of marriage is sinful. Just so, the Christian belongs completely to Jesus Christ; he is set apart for Him and Him alone. But he is also a part of a worldwide fellowship, the church, "all those everywhere who call on the name of our Lord Jesus Christ" (1:2). A defiled and unfaithful believer not only sins against the Lord, but he also sins against his fellow Christians.

> *"I appeal to you, brothers, in the name of our Lord Jesus Christ, that all of you agree with one another so that there may be no divisions among you and that you may be perfectly united in mind and thought"*
>
> *(1 Corinthians 1:10).*

Applying God's Truth:

1. Can you identify any ways that your church has deserted Jesus to pursue worldly interests?

2. On a personal level, are there any activities you need to give up in order to follow Jesus more completely?

3. How can the sin of one person affect the church as a whole?

DAY 3

Read 1 Corinthians 1:18-31

Low and Mighty

God chose the foolish, the weak, the lowly, and the despised to show the proud world their need and His grace. The lost world admires birth, social status, financial success, power, and recognition. But none of these things can guarantee eternal life.

The message and miracle of God's grace in Jesus Christ utterly puts to shame the high and mighty people of this world. The wise of this world cannot understand how God changes sinners into saints, and the mighty of this world are helpless to duplicate the miracle. God's "foolishness" confounds the wise; God's "weakness" confounds the mighty!

The annals of church history are filled with the accounts of great sinners whose lives were transformed by the power of the Gospel. In my own ministry, as in the ministry of most pastors and preachers, I have seen amazing things take place that the lawyers and psychologists could not understand. We have seen delinquent teenagers become successful students and useful citizens. We have seen marriages restored and homes reclaimed, much to the amazement of the courts.

> *"God chose the foolish things of the world to shame the wise; God chose the weak things of the world to shame the strong"*
> *(1 Corinthians 1:27).*

....

And why does God reveal the foolishness and the weakness of this present world system, even with its philosophy and religion? "So that no one may boast before Him" (v. 29). Salvation must be wholly of grace; otherwise, God cannot get the glory.

Applying God's Truth:

1. Can you think of a recent lesson you've learned from someone most people would consider foolish, weak, or lowly?

2. What is an amazing act of God you've witnessed lately that "confounds" those who are wise and/or powerful?

3. Are you content with being perceived by others as foolish and weak? Explain.

DAY 4

Read *1 Corinthians 2:1-5*

Mixed Messages

My wife was at the wheel of our car as we drove to Chicago, and I was in the co-pilot's seat reading the page proofs of another author's book that a publisher had asked me to review. Occasionally I would utter a grunt, and then a groan, and finally I shook my head and said, "Oh, no! I can't believe it!"

"I take it you don't like the book," she said. "Something wrong with it?"

"You bet there is!" I replied. "Just about everything is wrong with it, because this man does not know what the message of the Gospel really is!"

There was a time, however, when that author had been faithful to the Gospel. But over the years, he had begun to take a philosophical (and, I fear, political) approach to the Gospel. The result was a hybrid message that was no Gospel at all.

It is worth noting that when Paul ministered in Corinth, he obeyed our Lord's commission and preached the Gospel.

What had happened at Corinth is happening in churches today: men are mixing philosophy (man's

> *"I resolved to know nothing while I was with you except Jesus Christ and Him crucified"*
> *(1 Corinthians 2:2).*

wisdom) with God's revealed message, and this is causing confusion and division. Different preachers have their own "approach" to God's message, and some even invent their own vocabulary! Paul urged his readers to return to the fundamentals of the Gospel message.

Applying God's Truth:

1. In what ways do some people try to combine ungodly philosophies with the truth of the Gospel?

2. In what ways do some people try to combine a political agenda with the truth of the Gospel?

3. How can you stay focused on "Jesus Christ and Him crucified" without getting bogged down in politics and philosophy?

DAY 5

Read 1 Corinthians 2:6-10

Salvation: A United Effort

Our salvation involves all three Persons in the Godhead. You cannot be saved apart from the Father's electing grace, the Son's loving sacrifice, and the Spirit's ministry of conviction and regeneration. It is not enough to say, "I believe in God." What God? Unless it is "the God and Father of our Lord Jesus Christ" (Eph. 1:3), there can be no salvation.

This trinitarian aspect of our salvation helps us to understand better some of the mysteries of our salvation. Many people get confused (or frightened) when they hear about election and predestination. As far as the Father is concerned, I was saved when He chose me in Christ before the foundation of the world (Eph. 1:4), but I knew nothing about that the night I was saved! It was a hidden part of God's wonderful, eternal plan.

As far as God the Son is concerned, I was saved when He died for me on the cross. He died for the sins of the whole world, yet the whole world is not saved. This is where the Spirit comes in: as far as the Spirit is concerned, I was saved on May 12, 1945 at a Youth for Christ rally where I heard Billy Graham (then a young

> " 'No eye has seen, no ear has heard, no mind has conceived what God has prepared for those who love Him' — but God has revealed it to us by His Spirit"
>
> *(1 Corinthians 2:9-10).*

evangelist) preach the Gospel. It was then that the Holy Spirit applied the Word to my heart, I believed, and God saved me.

Applying God's Truth:

1. In what ways did you observe the activity of each member of the Godhead in regard to your salvation?

2. What would you consider a "hidden part of God's wonderful, eternal plan" for your own life?

3. Why do you think God allows salvation to be such a "mystery" to us?

DAY 6

Read *1 Corinthians 2:11-16*

Speaking the Language

Each of our four children has a different vocation. We have a pastor, a nurse, an electronics designer, and a secretary in a commercial real estate firm. Each of the children had to learn a specialized vocabulary in order to succeed. The only one I really understand is the pastor.

The successful Christian learns the vocabulary of the Spirit and makes use of it. He knows the meaning of justification, sanctification, adoption, propitiation, election, inspiration, and so forth. In understanding God's vocabulary, we come to understand God's Word and God's will for our lives. If the engineering student can grasp the technical terms of chemistry, physics, or electronics, why should it be difficult for Christians, taught by the Spirit, to grasp the vocabulary of Christian truth?

Yet I hear church members say, "Don't preach doctrine. Just give us heartwarming sermons that will encourage us!" Sermons based on what? If they are not based on doctrine, they will accomplish nothing! "But doctrine is so dull!" people complain. Not if it is presented the way the Bible presents it—doctrine to

> *"This is what we speak, not in words taught us by human wisdom but in words taught by the Spirit, expressing spiritual truths in spiritual words"*
>
> *(1 Corinthians 2:13).*

me is exciting! What a thrill to be able to study the Bible and let the Spirit teach us "the deep things of God" (1 Cor. 2:10).

Applying God's Truth:

1. How would you define the Christian concept of justification? Sanctification? Adoption? Propitiation? Election? Inspiration?

2. If your understanding of Christian doctrine isn't what you want it to be, how can you learn what you want to know?

3. As you learn "the vocabulary of the Spirit," do you foresee any potential problems with *using* Christian "lingo"? Explain.

DAY 7

Read 1 Corinthians 3:1-9

Watch Your Diet

What are the marks of maturity? For one thing, you can tell the mature person by *his diet*. As I write this chapter, we are watching our grandson and our granddaughter grow up. Becky is still being nursed by her mother, but Jonathan now sits at the table and uses his little cup and (with varying degrees of success) his tableware. As children grow, they learn to eat different food. They graduate from milk to meat.

What is the difference? The usual answer is that "milk" represents the easy things in the Word, while "solid food" (or "meat") represents the hard doctrines. But I disagree with that traditional explanation, and my proof is Hebrews 5:10-14. That passage seems to teach that "milk" represents what Jesus Christ did on earth, while "solid food" concerns what He is doing now in heaven. The writer of Hebrews wanted to teach his readers about the present heavenly priesthood of Jesus Christ, but his readers were so immature, he could not do it.

It is not difficult to determine a believer's spiritual maturity, or immaturity, if you discover what kind of "diet" he enjoys. The immature believer knows little

> *"I gave you milk, not solid food, for you were not yet ready for it. Indeed, you are still not ready. You are still worldly"*
> (1 Corinthians 3:2-3).

about the present ministry of Christ in heaven. He knows the *facts* about our Lord's life and ministry on earth, but not the *truths* about His present ministry in heaven. He lives on "Bible stories" and not Bible doctrines. He has no understanding of 1 Corinthians 2:6-7.

Applying God's Truth:

1. What food(s) would you say best represent(s) your current spiritual "diet"? Why?

2. If "milk" represents what Jesus did on earth and "meat" represents what He is doing now in heaven, which "food group" are you more familiar with? How can you get a better "balanced diet"?

3. Can you give a personal example about someone who knows spiritual "facts," but not necessarily "truths"?

DAY 8

Read *1 Corinthians 3:10-23*

Secrets of Church Success

Young ministers often asked Dr. Campbell Morgan the secret of his pulpit success. Morgan replied, "I always say to them the same thing—work; hard work; and again, work!" Morgan was in his study at 6 o'clock each morning, digging treasures out of the Bible. You can find wood, hay, and straw (v. 12) in your backyard, and it will not take too much effort to pick it up. But if you want gold, silver, and jewels, *you have to dig for them.* Lazy preachers and Sunday School teachers will have much to answer for at the Judgment Seat of Christ—and so will preachers and teachers who steal materials from others instead of studying and making it their own.

It comes as a shock to some church members that you cannot manage a local church the same way you run a business. This does not mean we should not follow good business principles, but the operation is totally different. There is a wisdom of this world that works for the world, but it will not work for the church.

The world depends on promotion, prestige, and the influence of money and important people. The church depends on prayer, the power of the Spirit, humility,

> *"Do not deceive yourselves. If any one of you thinks he is wise by the standards of this age, he should become a "fool" so that he may become wise"*
> *(1 Corinthians 3:18).*

sacrifice, and service. The church that imitates the world may seem to succeed in time, but it will turn to ashes in eternity.

Applying God's Truth:

1. What would you say best describes the type of "building" you've been doing on the spiritual foundation that Jesus has laid: straw, hay, wood, precious stones, silver, or gold? Explain.

2. What successful business principles do you think would work for the church? Which ones wouldn't?

3. In what ways do you try to help your church be the best it can be?

DAY 9

Read *1 Corinthians 4:1-13*

No Place for Pride

There is no place for pride in the ministry. If a truly great leader like Paul considered himself "on display at the end of the procession," where does this leave the rest of us? Church members are wrong when they measure ministers other than by the standards God has given. They are also wrong when they boast about their favorite preachers. This is not to say that faithful servants cannot be recognized and honored, but in all things, God must be glorified (1 Thes. 5:12-13).

Paul was a fool according to the standards of men. Had he remained a Jewish rabbi, he could have attained great heights in the Jewish religion (Gal 1:14). Or had he sided with the Jewish legalists in the Jerusalem church and not ministered to the Gentiles, he could have avoided a great deal of persecution (Acts 15; 21:17ff).

The Corinthians were wise in their own eyes, but they were actually fools in the sight of God. By depending on the wisdom and the standards of the world, they were acting like fools. The way to be spiritually wise is to become a fool in the eyes of the world (1 Cor. 3:18). I often find myself quoting those

> "It seems to me that God has put us apostles on display at the end of the procession, like men condemned to die in the arena. We have been made a spectacle to the whole universe, to angels as well as to men"
> *(1 Corinthians 4:9).*

....

words of martyred Jim Elliot: "He is no fool who gives what he cannot keep to gain what he cannot lose."

Applying God's Truth:

1. In what specific ways has pride damaged the church as a whole? How about your local church?

2. Do you think congregation members help contribute to the pride of some preachers? How might this potential problem be kept to a minimum?

3. What are some things you "cannot keep"? What are the things you "cannot lose"?

DAY 10

Read *1 Corinthians 4:14-21*

Discipline versus Disobedience

A child's will must be broken, but not destroyed. Until a colt is broken, it is dangerous and useless, but once it learns to obey, it becomes gentle and useful. Pride is a terrible thing in the Christian life and in the church. The yeast of sin (5:6-8) had made the Corinthians "puffed up," even to the point of saying, "Paul will not come to us! His bark is worse than his bite!" (See 2 Corinthians 10:8-11.)

Paul had been patient with their disobedience, but now he warned them that the time had come for discipline. Paul was not like the tolerant modern mother who shouted at her spoiled son, "This is the last time I'm going to tell you for the last time!"

A faithful parent must discipline his children. It is not enough to teach them and be an example before them; he must also punish them when they rebel and refuse to obey. Paul would have preferred to come with meekness and deal with their sins in a gentle manner, but their own attitude made this difficult. They were puffed up—and even proud of their disobedience! (5:1-2)

The contrast in this paragraph is between *speech* and *power*, words and deeds. The arrogant

> *"The kingdom of God is not a matter of talk but of power"*
> *(1 Corinthians 4:20).*

Corinthians had no problem "talking big," the way children often will do, but they could not back up their talk with their "walk." Their religion was only in words. Paul was prepared to back up his "talk" with power, with deeds that would reveal their sins and God's holiness.

Applying God's Truth:

1. At what point did you move from needing to be disciplined by others into taking responsibility for self-discipline?

2. How does lack of self-discipline among its members cause problems in *today's* church?

3. In what specific area(s) is it hardest to discipline yourself? How can you persevere even though it is difficult?

DAY 11

Read *1 Corinthians 5*

"Shape Up or Ship Out"

The people at Corinth were puffed up. They were boasting of the fact that their church was so "open-minded" that even fornicators could be members in good standing! The sin in question was a form of incest: a professed Christian (and a member of the church) was living with his stepmother in a permanent alliance. Since Paul does not pass judgment on the woman (vv. 9-13), we assume that she was not a member of the assembly and probably not even a Christian. This kind of sin was condemned by the Old Testament Law (Lev. 18:6-8; 20:11) as well as by the laws of the Gentile nations. Paul shamed the church by saying, "Even the unsaved Gentiles don't practice this kind of sin!"

While Christians are not to judge one another's motives or ministries, we are certainly expected to be honest about each other's conduct. In my own pastoral ministry, I have never enjoyed having to initiate church discipline, but since it is commanded in the Scriptures, we must obey God and set personal feelings aside.

Paul described here an official church meeting at which the offender was dealt with according to divine

> *"It is actually reported that there is sexual immorality among you, and of a kind that does not occur even among pagans: A man has his father's wife. And you are proud!"*
> *(1 Corinthians 5:1-2).*

instructions. Public sin must be publicly judged and condemned. The sin was not to be "swept under the rug"; for, after all, it was known far and wide even among the unsaved who were outside the church.

Applying God's Truth:

1. If you had been a member of the assembly at Corinth, how do you think you would have been affected by the blatant sin within the church?

2. What issues in today's church might attract similar attention from the secular world?

3. Do you have guidelines to determine when to: (1) Dismiss a problem as a "weaker brother" issue; (2) Forgive the sin and ignore it; or (3) See it as a danger and confront the person? If not, do you *need* guidelines?

DAY 12

Read 1 Corinthians 6:1-8

Loss Suits

The church at Corinth was rapidly losing its testimony in the city. Not only did the unsaved know about the immorality in the assembly, but they were also aware of the lawsuits involving members of the church. Not only were there sins of the flesh, but also sins of the spirit.

Paul detected three tragedies in this situation. First, *the believers were presenting a poor testimony to the lost.* Even the unbelieving Jews dealt with their civil cases in their own synagogue courts. To take the problems of Christians and discuss them before the "unjust" and "unbelievers" was to weaken the testimony of the Gospel.

Second, *the congregation had failed to live up to its full position in Christ.* Since the saints will one day participate in the judgment of the world and even of fallen angels, they ought to be able to settle their differences here on earth. The Corinthians boasted of their great spiritual gifts. Why, then, did they not use them in solving their problems?

There was a third tragedy: *the members suing*

> *"The very fact that you have lawsuits among you means you have been completely defeated already. Why not rather be wronged? Why not rather be cheated?"*
>
> *(1 Corinthians 6:7).*

each other had already lost. Even if some of them won their cases, they had incurred a far greater loss in their disobedience to the Word of God. Better to lose money or possessions than to lose a brother and lose your testimony too.

Applying God's Truth:

1. Do you think Paul's plea for Christians to avoid lawsuits between each other still applies? Why?

2. On a scale of 1 (least) to 10 (most), how much anger do you feel when someone takes advantage of you? How might the number eventually be lower?

3. Rather than secular lawsuits, what are some other options Christians today could pursue when they feel wronged by a fellow believer?

DAY 13

Read 1 Corinthians 6:9-20

The Best Sex

There is certainly excitement and enjoyment in sexual experience outside of marriage, *but there is not enrichment.* Sex outside of marriage is like a man robbing a bank: he gets something, but it is not his and he will one day pay for it. Sex within marriage can be like a person putting money into a bank: there is safety, security, and he will collect dividends.

Paul referred to the creation account (Gen. 2:24) to explain the seriousness of sexual sin. When a man and woman join their bodies, *the entire personality is involved.* There is a much deeper experience, a "oneness," that brings with it deep and lasting consequences. Paul warned that sexual sin is the most serious sin a person can commit against his body, for it involves the whole person.

Paul did not suggest that being joined to a harlot was the equivalent of marriage, for marriage also involves *commitment.* When two people pledge their love and faithfulness to each other, they lay a strong foundation on which to build. Marriage protects sex and enables the couple, committed to each other, to grow in this wonderful experience.

> *"Flee from sexual immorality. All other sins a man commits are outside his body, but he who sins sexually sins against his own body"*
>
> *(1 Corinthians 6:18).*

....

In my pastoral counseling, I have had to help married couples whose relationship was falling apart because of the consequences of premarital sex, as well as extramarital sex. The harvest of sowing to the flesh is sometimes delayed, but it is certain (Gal. 6:7-8). How sad it is to live with the consequences of *forgiven* sin.

Applying God's Truth:

1. In what ways is sex *enriched* through marriage? Explain.

2. How is premarital or extramarital sex a sin "against one's own body"?

3. Can you think of some specific situations where sexual sin was forgiven, yet the person(s) involved still had to "live with the consequences"?

DAY 14

Read *1 Corinthians 7:1-24*

A Better Yield

As in all things, the spiritual must govern the physical; for our bodies are God's temples. The husband and wife may abstain from sex in order to devote their full interest to prayer and fasting (7:5), but they must not use this as an excuse for prolonged separation. Paul is encouraging Christian partners to be "in tune" with each other in matters both spiritual and physical.

Not only did the church ask about celibacy, but they also asked Paul about divorce. If divorce does occur, the parties should remain unmarried or seek reconciliation. It has been my experience as a pastor that when a husband and wife are yielded to the Lord, and when they seek to please each other in the marriage relationship, the marriage will be so satisfying that neither partner would think of looking elsewhere for fulfillment.

"There are no sex problems in marriage," a Christian counselor once told me, "only personality problems with sex as one of the symptoms." The present frightening trend of increased divorces among Christians (and even among the clergy) must break the heart of God.

> *"The wife's body does not belong to her alone but also to her husband. In the same way, the husband's body does not belong to him alone but also to his wife"*
> *(1 Corinthians 7:4).*

Applying God's Truth:

1. For what reasons do you think married couples begin to withhold sex from each other? What are the potential consequences of doing so?

2. What signs do you detect in today's society that suggest husbands and wives aren't yielding to each other (and God) as they should?

3. What advice would you offer a Christian couple on the brink of divorce?

DAY 15

Read *1 Corinthians 7:25-40*

Making Marriage Last

It is God's will that the marriage union be permanent, a lifetime commitment. There is no place in Christian marriage for a "trial marriage," nor is there any room for the "escape-hatch" attitude: "If the marriage doesn't work, we can always get a divorce."

For this reason, marriage must be built on something sturdier than good looks, money, romantic excitement, and social acceptance. There must be Christian commitment, character, and maturity. There must be a willingness to grow, to learn from each other, to forgive and forget, to minister to one another.

Paul closed the section by telling the widows that they were free to marry, but the man "must belong to the Lord" (v. 39). This means that they must not only marry believers, but marry in the will of God. Paul's counsel was that they remain single, but he left the decision to them.

God has put "walls" around marriage, not to make it a prison, but to make it a safe fortress. The person who considers marriage a prison should not get

> *"A woman is bound to her husband as long as he lives. But if her husband dies, she is free to marry anyone she wishes, but he must belong to the Lord"*
> (1 Corinthians 7:39).

married. When two people are lovingly and joyfully committed to each other — and to their Lord — the experience of marriage is one of enrichment and enlargement. They grow together and discover the richness of serving the Lord as a "team" in their home and church.

Applying God's Truth:

1. Based on personal observations, what would you say are the most common reasons for divorce?

2. Now, thinking of the couples you know who have been together for a long time, what do you see as the "secret" of a strong marriage?

3. In what ways do you feel people today take marriage (and remarriage) too lightly?

DAY 16

Read 1 Corinthians 8

Puffy "I"s and "Know"s

Love and knowledge must go together. It has well been said, "Knowledge without love is brutality, but love without knowledge is hypocrisy." Paul's great concern was that the strong saints help the weaker saints to grow and to stop being weak saints. Some people have the false notion that the *strong* Christians are the ones who live by rules and regulations and who get offended when others exercise their freedom in Christ, but such is not the case. It is the *weak* Christians who must have the security of law and who are afraid to use their freedom in Christ. It is the weak Christians who are prone to judge and criticize stronger believers and to stumble over what they do. This, of course, makes it difficult for the strong saints to minister to their weaker brothers and sisters.

It is here that love enters the picture, for "love builds up" and puts others first. When spiritual knowledge is used in love, the stronger Christian can take the hand of the weaker Christian and help him to stand and walk so as to enjoy his freedom in Christ. *You cannot force-feed immature believers and transform them into giants.* Knowledge must be

> *"We know that we all possess knowledge. Knowledge puffs up, but love builds up"*
> *(1 Corinthians 8:1).*

mixed with love; otherwise, the saints will end up with "big heads" instead of enlarged hearts.

Applying God's Truth:

1. Do you know anyone who has "knowledge without love"? How about "love without knowledge"? How do you relate to such people?

2. How has someone used a combination of love and knowledge to make you a stronger Christian?

3. How are *you* using love and knowledge to help weaker Christians? Can you think of other people you know who could use some help?

DAY 17

Read *1 Corinthians 9:1-18*

Not in It for the Money

It is unfortunate when the ministry of the Gospel is sometimes hindered by an overemphasis on money. The unsaved world is convinced that most preachers and missionaries are only involved in "religious rackets" to take money from innocent people. No doubt there are religious "racketeers" in the world today—people who "use" religion to exploit others and control them. We would certainly not agree with their purposes or their practices. We must make sure that nothing we do in our own ministry gives the impression that we are of their number.

A wrong attitude toward money has hindered the Gospel from the earliest days of the church. Simon the magician thought he could buy the gift of the Spirit with money (Acts 8:18-24). Ananias and Sapphira loved money more than they loved the truth, and God killed them (Acts 5).

For eighteen fruitful years, Dr. H.A. Ironside pastored the Moody Church in Chicago. I recall the first time I heard him announce an offering. He said, "We ask God's people to give generously. If you are not a believer in Jesus Christ, we do not ask you to give. We

> *"What then is my reward? Just this: that in preaching the Gospel I may offer it free of charge, and so not make use of my rights in preaching it"*
> (1 Corinthians 9:18).

have a gift for you — eternal life through faith in Christ!" He made it clear that the offering was for believers, lest the unsaved in the congregation stumble over money and then reject the Gospel.

Applying God's Truth:

1. What are some misperceptions about the church formed by people who witness "religious racketeers"?

2. Do you think money should ever be discussed publicly at church? To what extent?

3. How can money propel the cause of the Gospel? How can it become a hindrance?

DAY 18

Read *1 Corinthians 9:19-27*

Run for Your (Spiritual) Life

An athlete must be disciplined if he is to win the prize. Discipline means giving up the good and the better for the best. The athlete must watch his diet as well as his hours. He must smile and say "No, thank you" when people offer him fattening desserts or invite him to late-night parties. There is nothing wrong with food or fun, but if they interfere with your highest goals, then they are hindrances and not helps.

The Christian does not run the race in order to get to heaven. He is in the race because he has been saved through faith in Jesus Christ.

In the same way, only Greek citizens were allowed to participate in the games, and they had to obey the rules both in their training and in their performing. Any contestant found breaking the training rules was automatically disqualified. The famous Indian athlete, Jim Thorpe, had to return his Olympic gold medals because the committee discovered he had previously played on a professional team.

In order to give up his rights and have the joy of winning lost souls, Paul had to discipline himself. That

> *"Run in such a way as to get the prize. Everyone who competes in the games goes into strict training. They do it to get a crown that will not last; but we do it to get a crown that will last forever"*
> *(1 Corinthians 9:24-25).*

is the emphasis of 1 Corinthians 9. Authority (rights) must be balanced by discipline. If we want to serve the Lord and win His reward and approval, we must pay the price.

Applying God's Truth:

1. In what ways has your spiritual life been like a race so far?

2. What do you expect to "win" when you get to the "finish line"?

3. Though "discipline" is often used in a negative context, how is it a positive attribute in sports and spiritual development?

DAY 19

Read 1 Corinthians 10

Inconsistently Consistent

Paul probably appeared inconsistent to those who did not understand his principles of Christian living. At times, he would eat what the Gentiles were eating. At other times, he would eat only "kosher" food with the Jews. But instead of being inconsistent, he was actually living *consistently* by the principles he laid down in these chapters of 1 Corinthians.

A weather vane seems inconsistent, first pointing in one direction and then in another. But a weather vane is always consistent: it always points toward the direction where the wind is blowing. That is what makes it useful.

As Christians we *do* have freedom. This freedom was purchased for us by Jesus Christ, so it is very precious. Freedom comes from knowledge: "You will know the truth, and the truth will set you free" (John 8:32). However, knowledge must be balanced by love; otherwise, it will tear down instead of build up.

The way we use our freedom and relate to others indicates whether we are mature in Christ. Strong and weak Christians need to work together in love to edify one another and glorify Jesus Christ.

> *" 'Everything is permissible'—but not everything is beneficial. 'Everything is permissible'—but not everything is constructive. Nobody should seek his own good, but the good of others"*
> *(1 Corinthians 10:23-24).*

Applying God's Truth:

1. Can you think of ways that obedience to God's commands may have made you appear inconsistent to other people from time to time?

2. Do you find it more comfortable to have hard and fast rules for behavior, or the freedom to be somewhat inconsistent? Explain.

3. In what ways can we misuse Christian freedom if we aren't careful?

DAY 20

Read *1 Corinthians 11:1-16*

Order in the Church

Eastern society at this time was very jealous over its women. Except for the temple prostitutes, the women wore long hair and, in public, wore a covering over their heads. (Paul did not use the word *veil,* i.e., a covering over the face. The woman put her regular shawl over her head, and this covering symbolized her submission and purity.) For the Christian women in the church to appear in public without the covering, let alone to pray and share the Word, was both daring and blasphemous.

Paul sought to restore order by reminding the Corinthians that God had made a difference between men and women, that each had a proper place in God's economy. There were also appropriate customs that symbolized these relationships and reminded both men and women of their correct places in the divine scheme. Paul did not say, or even hint, that *difference* meant *inequality* or *inferiority.* If there is to be peace in the church, then there must be some kind of order, and order of necessity involves rank. However, *rank* and *quality* are two different things. The captain has a higher rank than the private, but the private may be a better man.

> *"I want you to realize that the head of every man is Christ, and the head of the woman is man, and the head of Christ is God"*
>
> *(1 Corinthians 11:3).*

Applying God's Truth:

1. What are some of the expectations for the men and women in your church that help ensure order?

2. Considering that the worship service is only an hour or so out of a week, do you think it's wrong to submit your personal feelings to achieve order? Explain.

3. If someone feels inferior or unequal at church, what are his or her options?

DAY 21

Read *1 Corinthians 11:17-34*

Whose Supper Is This, Anyway?

Since the beginning of the church, it was customary for the believers to eat together (Acts 2:42, 46). It was an opportunity for fellowship and for sharing with those who were less privileged. No doubt they climaxed this meal by observing the Lord's Supper.

The "agape feast" (from the Greek word for "love") was part of the worship at Corinth, but some serious abuses had crept in. For one thing, there were various cliques in the church and people ate with their own "crowd" instead of fellowshiping with the whole church family.

Another fault was selfishness: the rich people brought a great deal of food for themselves while the poorer members went hungry. And some of the members were even getting drunk.

Of course, the divisions at the dinner were but evidence of the deeper problems in the church. The Corinthians thought they were advanced believers, when in reality they were but little children. Paul did not suggest that they abandon the feast, but rather that they restore its proper meaning. The "agape feast"

> ***"A man ought to examine himself before he eats of the bread and drinks of the cup"***
> *(1 Corinthians 11:28).*

should have been an opportunity for edification, but they were using it as a time for embarrassment.

Applying God's Truth:

1. Do you recognize any of these early church problems (or similar ones) in your own church "fellowships"?

2. What would you suggest to make your church meetings more edifying for all people involved?

3. How might your "regular" meetings bring more glory to God?

DAY 22

Read *1 Corinthians 12*

Body Building

Diversity in the body is an evidence of the wisdom of God. Each member needs the other members, and no member can afford to become independent. When a part of the human body becomes independent, you have a serious problem that could lead to sickness and even death. In a healthy human body, the various members cooperate with each other and even compensate for each other when a crisis occurs. The instant any part of the body says to any other part, "I don't need you!" it begins to weaken and die and create problems for the whole body.

A famous preacher was speaking at a ministers' meeting, and he took time before and after the meeting to shake hands with the pastors and chat with them. A friend asked him, "Why take time for a group of men you may never see again?" The world-renowned preacher smiled and said, "Well, I may be where I am because of them! Anyway, if I didn't need them on the way up, I might need them on the way down!" No Christian servant can say to any other servant, "My ministry can get along without you!"

> *"If one part [of the body] suffers, every part suffers with it; if one part is honored, every part rejoices with it"*
> *(1 Corinthians 12:26).*

Applying God's Truth:

1. In terms of a human body, what "part" would you say you are in the church? Why?

2. What is a recent situation where you suffered because someone else was suffering? When have you rejoiced because someone else was joyful?

3. Who are some people you've been trying to "get along without" whom you ought to start to work *with* instead?

DAY 23

Read 1 Corinthians 13

Not Enough Love?

It was Jonathan Swift, the satirical author of *Gulliver's Travels*, who said, "We have just enough religion to make us hate, but not enough to make us love one another." Spiritual gifts, no matter how exciting and wonderful, are useless and even destructive if they are not ministered in love. In all three of the "body" passages in Paul's letters, there is an emphasis on love. The main evidence of maturity in the Christian life is a growing love for God and for God's people, as well as a love for lost souls. It has well been said that love is the "circulatory system" of the body of Christ.

Few chapters in the Bible have suffered more misinterpretation and misapplication than 1 Corinthians 13. Divorced from its context, it becomes "a hymn to love" or a sentimental sermon on Christian brotherhood. Many people fail to see that Paul was still dealing with the Corinthians' problems when he wrote these words: the abuse of the gift of tongues, division in the church, envy of others' gifts, selfishness (remember the lawsuits?), impatience with one another in the public meetings, and behavior that was disgracing the Lord.

> *"If I give all I possess to the poor and surrender my body to the flames, but have not love, I gain nothing"*
> (1 Corinthians 13:3).

The only way spiritual gifts can be used creatively is when Christians are motivated by love.

Applying God's Truth:

1. Can you think of people who try to use spiritual gifts without being loving as well? What do you think of their ministries?

2. Do you think love is sweet and natural, or difficult and rare? Explain.

3. Of all of your current relationships and situations, where would you say love is most needed?

DAY 24

Read *1 Corinthians 14:1-25*

Do You Understand?

A ministry that does not build up will tear down, no matter how "spiritual" it may seem. When we explain and apply the Word of God to individual lives, we have a ministry of edification. In this section, Paul repeatedly showed concern for *understanding*. It is not enough for the minister to impart information to people; the people must *receive* it if it is to do them any good. The seed that is received in the good ground is the seed that bears fruit, but this means that there must be an *understanding* of the Word of God (Matt. 13:23). If a believer wants to be edified, he must prepare his heart to receive the Word (1 Thes. 2:13). Not everybody who *listens* really *hears*.

The famous Congregational minister, Dr. Joseph Parker, preached at an important meeting and afterward was approached by a man who criticized a minor point in the sermon. Parker listened patiently to the man's criticism, and then asked, "And what *else* did you get from the message?" This remark simply withered the critic, who then disappeared into the crowd. Too often we are quick to judge the sermon instead of allowing the Word of God to judge us.

> *"Follow the way of love and eagerly desire spiritual gifts"*
> *(1 Corinthians 14:1).*

....

Applying God's Truth:

1. In what ways have people "built you up" this week? What opportunities did they miss?

2. When have you recently been guilty of listening without hearing?

3. What are three things you can do to try to be a more understanding person from now on? Specifically, how can you better understand people who don't agree with you on the issue of speaking in tongues?

DAY 25

Read *1 Corinthians 14:26-35*

Group Consideration

We must use the Word of God to test every message that we hear, asking the Spirit to guide us. There are false teachers in the world and we must beware. But even true teachers and preachers do not know everything and sometimes make mistakes. Each listener must evaluate the message and apply it to his own heart.

Our public meetings are more formal than those of the early church, so it is not likely that we need to worry about the order of the service. But in our more informal meetings, we need to consider one another and maintain order. I recall being in a testimony meeting where a woman took forty minutes telling a boring experience and, as a result, destroyed the spirit of the meeting.

Evangelist D.L. Moody was leading a service and asked a man to pray. Taking advantage of his opportunity, the man prayed on and on. Sensing that the prayer was killing the meeting instead of blessing it, Moody spoke up and said, "While our brother finishes his prayer, let us sing a hymn!" Those who are in charge of public meetings need to have discernment — and courage.

"God is not a God of disorder but of peace"
(1 Corinthians 14:33).

Applying God's Truth:

1. If you were a professional church consultant, what objective suggestions would you give your pastor for how to improve your church worship services?

2. Do people at your church tend to abuse the privilege of participating in public worship? Do you think they should be tolerated or confronted? Why?

3. In what ways do you think your church leaders need to have clearer discernment? Additional courage?

DAY 26

Read **1 Corinthians 14:36-40**

A Tongues Summary

It might be helpful to summarize what Paul wrote about the gift of tongues. It is the God-given ability to speak in a known language with which the speaker was not previously acquainted. The purpose was not to win the lost, but to edify the saved. Not every believer had this gift, nor was this gift an evidence of spirituality or the result of a "baptism of the Spirit."

Only three persons were permitted to speak in tongues in one meeting, and they had to do so in order and with interpretation. If there was no interpreter, they had to keep silent. Prophecy is the superior gift, but tongues were not to be despised if they were exercised according to Scripture.

When the foundational work of the apostles and prophets ended, it would seem that the gifts of knowledge, prophecy, and tongues would no longer be needed. "Where there are tongues, they will be stilled" (13:8). Certainly God could give this gift today if He pleased, but I am not prepared to believe that every instance of tongues today is divinely energized. Nor would I go so far as to say that all instances of tongues are either satanic or self-induced.

> *"Everything should be done in a fitting and orderly way"*
> *(1 Corinthians 14:40).*

....

It is unfortunate when believers make tongues a test of fellowship or spirituality. That in itself would alert me that the Spirit would not be at work. Let's keep our priorities straight and major on winning the lost and building the church.

Applying God's Truth:

1. Do you have any questions about the gift of tongues? If so, where can you go to find answers?

2. What do you think 1 Corinthians 13:8 means: "Where there are tongues, they will be stilled"?

3. Why do you think Paul gave so many instructions regarding the proper procedures for speaking in tongues?

DAY 27

Read *1 Corinthians 15:1-28*

Paul's Witness

One of the greatest witnesses of the resurrection was Paul himself, for as an unbeliever he was soundly convinced that Jesus was dead. The radical change in his life—a change which brought him persecution and suffering—is certainly evidence that the Lord had indeed been raised from the dead. Paul made it clear that his salvation was purely an act of God's grace, but that grace worked in and through him as he served the Lord.

At this point, Paul's readers would say, "Yes, we agree that *Jesus* was raised from the dead." Then Paul would reply, "If you believe that, then you must believe in the resurrection of *all* the dead!" Christ came as a man, truly human, and experienced all that we experience, except that He never sinned. If there is no resurrection, then Christ was not raised. If He was not raised, there is no Gospel to preach. If there is no Gospel, then you have believed in vain and you are still in your sins! If there is no resurrection, then believers who have died have no hope. We shall never see them again!

The conclusion is obvious: Why be a Christian if we have only suffering in this life and no future glory to

> *"[Jesus] appeared to James, then to all the apostles, and last of all He appeared to me also, as to one abnormally born. For I am the least of the apostles and do not even deserve to be called an apostle"*
> *(1 Corinthians 15:8-9).*

anticipate? (In verses 29-34, Paul expanded this idea.) The resurrection is not just important; it is "of first importance" (v. 3), because all that we believe hinges upon it.

Applying God's Truth:

1. Is the resurrection of the dead "of first importance" to you? Give an example.

2. What would you tell a friend who asked, "How do you think you're going to be different after your resurrection?"

3. Can people look at the changes you've made in your life and see God's grace? Why or why not?

DAY 28

Read *1 Corinthians 15:29-58*

Victory: Now and Later

The heavenly kingdom is not made for the kind of bodies we now have, bodies of flesh and blood. So when Jesus returns, the bodies of living believers will instantly be transformed to be like His body (1 John 3:1-3), and the dead believers shall be raised with new, glorified bodies. Our new bodies will not be subject to decay or death.

Sigmund Freud, the founder of psychiatry, wrote: "And finally there is the painful riddle of death, for which no remedy at all has yet been found, nor probably ever will be." Christians have victory *in* death and *over* death! Why? Because of the victory of Jesus Christ in His own resurrection. Jesus said: "Because I live, you also will live" (John 14:19).

We share the victory *today*. The literal translation of verse 57 is, "But thanks be to God *who keeps on giving us the victory* through our Lord Jesus Christ." We experience "the power of His resurrection" in our lives as we yield to Him (Phil. 3:10). Verse 58 is Paul's hymn of praise to the Lord as well as his closing admonition to the church. Because of the assurance of Christ's victory over death, we know that nothing we

> *"Thanks be to God! He gives us the victory through our Lord Jesus Christ"*
> *(1 Corinthians 15:57).*

do for Him will ever be wasted or lost. We can be steadfast in our service, unmovable in suffering, abounding in ministry to others, because we know our labor is not in vain.

Applying God's Truth:

1. What are your fears and concerns about death?

2. In what ways has Jesus provided victory in regard to the things you just listed?

3. In what other areas do you need to experience victory? What steps do you need to take toward more complete victory in your spiritual struggles?

DAY 29

Read *1 Corinthians 16:1-9*

Doctrine and Duty

It is unfortunate when Christian ministries lose their testimony because they mismanage funds entrusted to them. Every ministry ought to be businesslike in its financial affairs. Paul was very careful not to allow anything to happen that would give his enemies opportunity to accuse him of stealing funds (2 Cor. 8:20-21).

This explains why Paul encouraged the *churches* to share in the offering and to select dependable representatives to help manage it. Paul was not against *individuals* giving personally; in this chapter he named various individuals who assisted him personally. This no doubt included helping him with his financial needs. But generally speaking, Christian giving is church-centered. Many churches encourage their members to give designated gifts through the church treasury.

It is interesting that Paul mentioned the offering just after his discussion about the resurrection. There were no "chapter breaks" in the original manuscripts, so the readers would go right from Paul's hymn of victory into his discussion about money. Doctrine and

> *"On the first day of every week, each one of you should set aside a sum of money in keeping with his income, saving it up, so that when I come no collections will have to be made"*
> *(1 Corinthians 16:2).*

....

duty go together; so do worship and works. Our giving is "not in vain" because our Lord is alive. It is His resurrection power that motivates us to give and to serve.

Applying God's Truth:

1. What connection do you see between Jesus' resurrection and your giving to the church?

2. What procedures does your church have to make sure money is not mismanaged?

3. Do you think monetary giving is all that is required of us, or do you think Paul's guidelines might apply to other kinds of giving as well? Explain.

DAY 30

Read *1 Corinthians 16:10-24*

In Conclusion...

Paul's closing words need not detain us. The "holy kiss" (16:20) was a common mode of greeting, the men kissing the men and the women kissing the women. If Paul were writing to Western churches, he would say, "Shake hands with one another."

Paul usually dictated his letters and then took the pen and added his signature. He also added his "benediction of grace" as a mark that the letter was authentic. The word *anathema* (v. 22, KJV) is Aramaic and means "accursed." Not to love Christ means not to believe in Him, and unbelievers are accursed (John 3:16-21). The word *maranatha* (v. 22, KJV) is Greek and means "our Lord comes" or (as a prayer) "our Lord, come!" If a person loves Jesus Christ, he will also love His appearing (2 Tim. 4:8).

Paul had been stern with the Corinthian believers, but he closed his letter by assuring them of his love. After all, "Wounds from a friend can be trusted" (Prov. 27:6).

Paul has shared a great deal of spiritual wisdom with us. May we receive it with meekness and put it into practice to the glory of God!

> *"Be on your guard; stand firm in the faith; be men of courage; be strong. Do everything in love"*
>
> *(1 Corinthians 16:13-14).*

Applying God's Truth:

1. Does your church have a special or unique type of greeting? If not, do you think it could use one?

2. If you had been a first-century Christian reading this epistle for the first time, what questions do you think you might have had for Paul?

3. What three noteworthy things have you learned (or been reminded of) from 1 Corinthians?